# Treetop Trauma

D1079543

# Treetop Trauma

## Robin and Chris Lawrie

Illustrated by
### Robin Lawrie

## Acknowledgements
The authors and publishers would like to thank Julia Francis,
Hereford Diocesan Deaf Church lay co-chaplain, for her help
with the sign language in the *Chain Gang* books, and
Dr Cathy Turtle, ecologist, for her help with the selection
of species in books 13 to 18.


Published by Evans Brothers Limited
2A Portman Mansions
Chiltern Street
London W1U 6NR

Printed in Hong Kong

**British Library Cataloguing in Publication data.**
Lawrie, Robin
  Treetop Trauma. – (The Chain Gang)
  1. Slam Duncan (Fictitious character) – Juvenile fiction
  2. All terrain cycling – Juvenile fiction 3. Adventure stories
  4. Children's stories
  I. Title II. Lawrie, Chris
  823.9'14[J]

ISBN 0 237 52564X

A property developer plans to build twenty houses right across our best downhill courses on Westridge, a hill behind our village. Westridge is where we practise and race, but maybe not for much longer.

*I'm Andy. (Andy is deaf and signs.)

We'd been working hard getting people to sign a petition against the development of our hill, but time was running out.

Not 'sittin', you daft banana, a SIT-IN! We sit down in front of the developers' bulldozers and phone the newspaper.

The newspaper sends a photographer, we get on the front page, and everybody will want to sign our petition.

Great idea, Slam, but there's no way I'm sitting down in front of bulldozers.

It's hopeless anyway. They're starting work on three houses next week.

THAT'S IT!

What?

TREE HOUSES. We'll do our sit-in in a tree house. We'll be safe up high.

*Nor me.

7

There were only two days until the last race of the season but we decided that our petition was more important. Lots of people would sign on race day.

We chose our tree.

We got to work.

It wasn't long before . . .

11

Then Dozy hung the trike under
the tree house . . .

12

. . . and hung a sign
under the trike.
It was black so we
couldn't read it until
Dozy got on the trike
and started to pedal,
which turned the dynamo,
making electricity, which lit up the sign.

We were all set for some free publicity!

Back in the tree house, Dozy made a call.

Hello, news desk? Shredshire Star? We're trying to save Westridge from developers. We're having a sit-in in a tree that they're going to cut down on Monday.

Then Dozy said:

We're also having a hunger strike.

WHAT!!

ITS OUR HILL       NO HOUSES ON WESTRIDGE

He had some
explaining
to do when
he finished the call!

When the photographer arrived, Dozy got on the trike and started pedalling.

The photographer took lots of shots.

15

The headline in the evening paper
looked great.

We had a great view
of the racing . . .

. . . Fionn collected lots of signatures and
we forgot to be hungry.

But then, around lunchtime, attracted by
the petition-signing crowd . . .

. . . the burger van pulled up under our tree.

It was TORTURE!

The smell was more than we could stand.

Dozy went down, spoke to Fionn . . .

. . . and gave her some money.

Twenty minutes later . . .

Dozy, it seemed, had gone mad. He began
yelling at Fionn to send up
the first aid box. Very
strange. We could see
no cuts, no blood,
nothing.

It was a very heavy first aid box that

Fionn brought up
the ladder. It also
smelled very
interesting.

It turned out to be full of . . .

. . . BURGERS AND CHIPS!

But our joy was short-lived.

It was our old racing rival, Punk Tuer.

The crowd melted away like snow in springtime. The burgers tasted like sawdust. Plus we had to watch Punk get the fastest time of the day.

It all felt pretty pointless. But the tree fellers would be there in the morning, together with the newspaper reporters, so we hung on through another rough night. But at 5 a.m. the police arrived.

We had all had enough anyway.

They were, too, as well as a reporter and
photographer from the Shredshire Star.

Before the tree got the chop our
tree house had to be pulled down.
A big crane dropped a hook
on it and began to tug.

We began to shout.

But with Andy being deaf, it was pointless.

He soon came down anyway . . .

. . . the hard way.

Andy was flopping around in the little pond behind the tree. The police rushed to help, but Larry was more interested in something wriggly in the grass.

The Star's reporter was curious, too.

That's a great crested newt.

Wow, triturus cristatus. Very rare. It must have been splashed out of the pond.

You seem to know your stuff. What else is up here that's rare?

Here, I'll show you.

So off we went. In the day we saw . . .

Then in the evening . . .

We all did.

On Monday,

Tuesday,

Wednesday,

Thursday.
Then, finally. . .

* Nice one!

Saturday.

We had saved the hill, and the wildlife!